See Like Me

Diana Noonan

This is a bee.

This is an owl.

This is a fly.

This is a dog.

I look at a flower.
This is what I see.

A bee looks at a flower.
This is what it sees.

I look at a mouse.
This is what I see.

An owl looks at a mouse.
This is what it sees.

I look at a cake.
This is what I see.

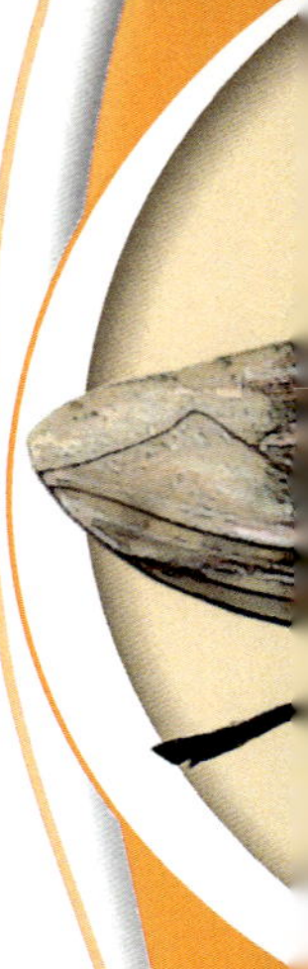

A fly looks at a cake.
This is what it sees.

I look at my dad.
This is what I see.

My dog looks at my dad.
This is what it sees.

I see 

A bee sees 

I see 

An owl sees 

I see 

A fly sees 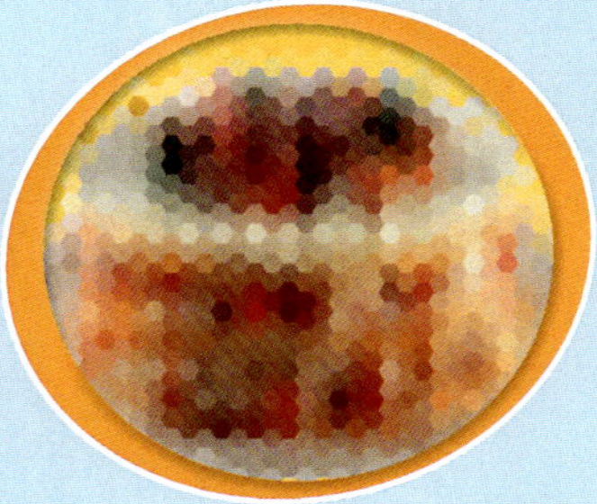

I see 

A dog sees